CW01512896

Original title:

Xanthic Pips Inside the Dragon Jute

Author: Mirell Mesipuu

ISBN HARDBACK: 978-1-80563-448-5

ISBN PAPERBACK: 978-1-80564-969-4

# Fables Weaved in Glittering Threads

In twilight's embrace, secrets hum,
Whispers of tales, where shadows come.
Threads of light in the fabric spin,
Crafting the worlds where dreams begin.

With flickering hopes, the stars align,
Each woven story, a spark divine.
In every heart, a fable sleeps,
Waiting for night, when magic creeps.

Through ebbing tides of forgotten lore,
Heroes rise and giants soar.
With every stitch, a truth is penned,
A tapestry wrought, where wishes blend.

In the quiet woods, the fairies play,
Casting spells while the moonlight sways.
With laughter spun in golden threads,
A legacy of dreams, where hope treads.

So sit by the fire, and let it glow,
Listen to tales of long ago.
For in each story, a shimmer we find,
Fables are woven, transcending time.

# Heartfelt Gleams in the Mists of Enchantment

In the mists where the soft winds sigh,
Whispers of love twinkle in the sky.
Moonbeams dance on the heart's delight,
Guiding lost souls, through the night.

A flicker of warmth, a gentle touch,
Hearts entwined, they long for much.
Each shared glance, a brush of fate,
In silent realms, they resonate.

With every wish upon a star,
They stitch together worlds from afar.
In shadows deep, true love will glow,
A heartfelt gleam, a steady flow.

Through emerald forests, their laughter rings,
A symphony sweet, where joy takes wings.
With every heartbeat, their spirits soar,
In enchanted realms, they crave for more.

As dawn breaks forth, the mists will part,
Revealing the treasures of each true heart.
In every tear, a tale unfolds,
Of love eternal, and courage bold.

## Gem-Laden Tales in the Loom of Dreams

In the loom of dreams, where visions gleam,
Gem-laden tales unfurl like a stream.
Each bead of light, a story untold,
Whispers of wonders, both meek and bold.

Through twilight's shimmer, a path appears,
An invitation to face our fears.
With every turn, a fortune found,
A tapestry rich, where joys abound.

Adorned with hope, the woven strands
Carry the touch of gentle hands.
In every thread, a promise glows,
Of hidden treasures the heart bestows.

So gather 'round, let the tales begin,
Of daring adventures and the strength within.
In this enchanted space, we weave our fate,
Jewel-encrusted dreams, we celebrate.

As morning dawns, the gems ignite,
Shimmering truths in the soft sunlight.
In the loom of dreams, we find our way,
Gem-laden tales, forever to stay.

# The Lure of Golden Wishes in Dusty Trails

In a world where whispers roam,
Golden wishes call you home.
Through the dust on winding ways,
Lies the magic of brighter days.

With each step, the heartbeats rise,
Hidden truths beneath blue skies.
Footprints tell of dreams once sown,
In the warmth of the unknown.

Beneath the stars, a shimmer bright,
Guides our path with softest light.
Trust the voices, let them lead,
To the place where hearts are freed.

In the glow of twilight's grace,
Feel the thrill of every chase.
Hope ignites, like fires in night,
Filling souls with pure delight.

When the journey's dream is cast,
Hold on tight, let none be lost.
For the lure that beckons near,
Whispers tales you long to hear.

## Sparkling Dreams in the Hearth of Night

In the hearth, the embers gleam,
Crafting visions from a dream.
Whispers dance on moonlit air,
Magic swirls, beyond compare.

Each flicker tells a story bold,
Of hopes and fears, both young and old.
Night unfolds with silken grace,
As starlit wishes find their place.

Gaze into the sparkles bright,
Chasing shadows, welcoming night.
Every shadow holds a gift,
In twilight's glow, our spirits lift.

Woven tales in dark and light,
Create a tapestry of night.
With every breath, let dreams ignite,
In the hearth, our hearts take flight.

For in this time, all troubles cease,
When hope and dreams embrace in peace.
Catch the sparks, let visions soar,
In the magic, we seek more.

## Beneath the Shadows, a Gilded Dance

Under shadows, silence reigns,
Gilded glimmers break the chains.
With each sway, a breath of fate,
In the dark, our dreams await.

Whispers swirl like leaves in breeze,
Cradling secrets with such ease.
Feel the pulse of haunting tunes,
As the night reveals its runes.

Draped in velvet, night unfolds,
Tales of courage, brave and bold.
Footsteps echo soft and low,
Beneath the moon's gentle glow.

Every flicker, every glance,
Sparks a wild and winding dance.
In this realm where shadows play,
Hearts entwine in soft ballet.

So let your spirit take a chance,
Join the shadows in their dance.
For beneath the stars above,
Lies the melody of love.

## Glowing Kernels of Fabled Fire

In the garden, knowledge grows,
Glowing kernels that life shows.
From the soil, a spark ignites,
Chasing dreams, embracing heights.

Find the fire within the heart,
In every ember, play your part.
Circled 'round by tales we weave,
Hope and joy will never leave.

Windows open to the sky,
As the fabled moments fly.
Feel the warmth of ancient lore,
Spreading light forevermore.

Let the flames of passion blaze,
Guide our paths through winding ways.
Glow with strength, let shadows fade,
In the light, our fears evade.

So gather 'round the fireside bright,
Where dreams take flight in starry night.
With glowing kernels, hearts inspire,
Igniting our eternal fire.

# Fruits of Dawn in Mystic Gardens

In mystic gardens where dreams unfold,
The fruits of dawn in glimmers of gold.
Petals whisper secrets, colors bright,
Beneath the dew, the world feels light.

Sunrise splashes the sky with hues,
Awakening life, a vibrant muse.
Winds carry laughter, sweetened air,
As creatures stir from slumber's lair.

Blissful songs in chorus rise,
Nature's magic fills the skies.
Each blossom tells a tale anew,
A dance of shadows, a playful view.

In twilight's embrace, the colors blend,
Through arches of leaves, the paths extend.
Gathered whispers of the earth,
Unravel the secrets of rebirth.

The fruits of dawn, so soft and fair,
Awake in gardens beyond compare.
With every breath, life's dreams ignite,
In mystic gardens, day takes flight.

# The Dragon's Hidden Luster

In caves of stone, where shadows creep,
A dragon stirs from ancient sleep.
Scales like gemstones, gleaming bright,
Shimmer in the dimming light.

Wings unfurl with a thunderous sound,
Earth shakes lightly, all around.
Fires flicker with a magical glow,
Secrets of ages, lost in the flow.

Guarded treasures of legends spun,
Stories of battles lost and won.
Within the depths, a heart of flame,
Echoes softly the dragon's name.

With every roar, the night ignites,
Stars above as precious sights.
The hidden luster of dreams proclaimed,
In hallowed halls where glory's claimed.

Beneath the moon's watchful gaze,
The dragon dances in twilight's haze.
A guardian fierce, yet wise and true,
With tales to share and skies so blue.

# Glimmers in the Woven Mist

In woven mist where whispers play,
Glimmers of magic hold sway.
Softly dancing, shadows entwine,
Between the worlds, a line divine.

Veils of fog and twilight's kiss,
Guide the wanderers into bliss.
Every step, a breath of peace,
In this realm, all troubles cease.

Mirrors of light, reflections rare,
Reveal the stories hidden there.
Ancient echoes of the past,
In every glance, a spell is cast.

Glimmers sparkling like starlit dew,
Painting wonders in every hue.
With every heartbeat, time suspends,
In woven mist where magic blends.

Gentle fingers of the breeze,
Carry secrets among the trees.
In twilight's realm, the heart will soar,
Glimmers in the mist, forevermore.

## Twists of Citrus in Dragon's Breath

In gardens lush where secrets lie,
Twists of citrus catch the eye.
Oranges glow like suns at dawn,
In the dragon's breath, they are drawn.

Leaves whisper tales of ages past,
With every gust, the shadows cast.
Fruity scents in the misty air,
Awaken magic beyond compare.

Sweetness mingles with a hint of fire,
In every bite, a heart's desire.
Juicy treasures, vibrant delight,
In the dragon's realm, all feels right.

The world erupts in colors bright,
As day surrenders to the night.
Citrus twists in a dance of fate,
In the dragon's breath, they celebrate.

With laughter ringing through the glade,
The citrus fruits and magic made.
In this wonder, hearts confess,
A life enchanted, we are blessed.

## The Shimmering Heart of a Velvet Flame

In twilight's grasp, the embers glow,
A dance of shadows, secrets flow.
A velvet flame, soft and bright,
Whispers tales of magic's light.

Soft heartbeats in the evening air,
A promise wrapped in tender care.
In flickers bold, the dreams ignite,
Guiding souls through starry night.

From depths of dusk, the courage wakes,
To face the fears as dawnlight breaks.
A shimmering heart, pure and true,
In the stillness, hope renews.

# Gilded Whispers in the Ancient Woods

In ancient woods where shadows weave,
The secrets whisper, none believe.
Gilded leaves on branches sway,
Echoes of a long-lost day.

Beneath the boughs, a fable dreams,
Where sunlight plays in golden beams.
With every rustle, stories fade,
In nature's cloak, their magic laid.

Forgotten paths where spirits roam,
Gilded whispers call them home.
Each step we take, a tale reborn,
In wooded realms, where dreams are worn.

## Nurturing Light in a Dragon's Nest

In caverns deep, where shadows sleep,
A dragon's nest holds secrets steep.
Nurturing light in scales that gleam,
Ignites the hearts of every dream.

Embers crackle, tales unfold,
Of fearless knights and treasures bold.
In fiery breaths, a lullaby,
Whispers of love that never die.

Each hatchling born in warmth and grace,
Finds tender light in velvet space.
With wings of dreams, they soar and race,
Through sky and time, they find their place.

## Golden Echoes from Mythic Roots

In golden echoes, legends rise,
From ancient roots, beneath the skies.
With every leaf, a story told,
In whispered tones of lore and gold.

Moonlit paths lead us away,
To realms where shadows dance and play.
Each heartbeat feels the ancient hum,
Of spirits lost, yet never numb.

In timeless grace, the past entwines,
As golden echoes, fate aligns.
With every breath, we draw the light,
From mythic roots, we take our flight.

# Threads of Gold in the Den of Secrets


In shadows deep where whispers weave,
A tapestry of tales conceived.
Each thread a spark, a journey bold,
Unraveled dreams in threads of gold.

With secrets spun in silent night,
The heartbeats pulse in muted light.
A labyrinth of mysteries unfold,
Where fortunes gleam in threads of gold.

Beneath the weight of whispered lies,
The truth will sing as darkness sighs.
An echo calls from ages old,
Awakening the threads of gold.

In every seam, a story's grace,
A dance of fate in this sacred space.
The hands of time, relentless, bold,
Unraveling the threads of gold.

So tread with care, o wanderer dear,
For every thread holds joy and fear.
In the den, where shadows scold,
Discover life in threads of gold.

# The Enchanted Grit of Harvested Dreams

In fields where starlight gently gleams,
The soil hums with whispered dreams.
Each grain a wish, a season's pluck,
The enchanted grit of harvest luck.

With hands outstretched, the toil begins,
To gather hopes where life still spins.
The dance of earth in tender streams,
We sow our hearts in harvested dreams.

A breeze of fate through golden loam,
Spreads seeds of joy, where wild things roam.
In every furrow, laughter beams,
Awakening the enchanted dreams.

With every dawn, the chorus plays,
A hymn to toil through sunlit days.
For what we reap, our spirit redeems,
The magic brewed in harvested dreams.

So take a moment, breathe it in,
The earthy scent of where we've been.
In fields of hope, life's web redeems,
The enchanted grit of harvested dreams.

# Veins of Sunlight through the Living Yarn

In fabrics rich with stories spun,
Where sunlight dances, life's begun.
Each fiber woven tight and strong,
Veins of sunlight hum a song.

The loom of time, a dance divine,
Crafts vibrant tales in every line.
The colors blend in rhythmic charm,
Veins of sunlight weave the calm.

Through shadows long, the patterns shift,
In every weave, a precious gift.
The tapestry of dreams, a balm,
Veins of sunlight keep us warm.

A whisper stirs in threads of night,
Awakening the deep-rooted light.
A journey flows, a winding arm,
Veins of sunlight hold the charm.

So take a thread, weave it tight,
In every heart lies woven light.
Embrace the warmth, let fears disarm,
Veins of sunlight through the living yarn.

## Hidden Radiance of Forgotten Legends

In whispered woods where shadows play,
The echoes of the past hold sway.
Among the leaves, the stories start,
Hidden radiance of the heart.

With ancient roots and weathered bark,
The legends flicker, a vital spark.
In twilight's glow, their voices chart,
The hidden radiance of the heart.

A firefly's glow in the midnight gloom,
Each flicker tells of joy and doom.
As ages pass, their truths impart,
Hidden radiance, a timeless art.

The moonlight weaves through branches bare,
Awakening dreams that linger there.
In every sigh, a whispered part,
The hidden radiance of the heart.

So listen close, let silence sing,
For in the stillness, legends cling.
To find what binds, where dreams depart,
Hidden radiance of the heart.

## Shimmering Treasures in a Woven World

In the heart of the forest, secrets dwell,
Whispers of magic, a soft, gentle spell.
Glimmers of gold in the leaves above,
Nature's own riches, a tapestry of love.

Every thread a story, vibrant and bright,
Stitched by the moon and kissed by the light.
Bridges of dreams span the winding brook,
Woven with wonder, from every nook.

Beneath the old oak, the children play near,
Hoping for luck in the games they hold dear.
A twinkle of promise in each playful glance,
Shimmering treasures invite them to dance.

With every new dawn, the colors arise,
Painted with whispers from the wise skies.
In the woven world, so magical, true,
The treasures of life wait for me and you.

As night cloaks the realm in starlit embrace,
Dreams turn to visions, in time and in space.
Each glint of a star is a tale yet untold,
In shimmering treasures, we're never too old.

# The Glow of Fortune within Fables Untold

Beneath the old tales where legends sleep,
Fortune shines softly, in secrets we keep.
A flicker of hope in the shadows so vast,
Promises echo from moments long past.

In the pages of fables, where heroes reside,
The glow of good fortune is hard to hide.
Woven through words, the magic can flow,
Each story a journey, a chance to grow.

With a heart full of dreams, we venture aboard,
Navigating the fate that the fates have stored.
Through valleys and peaks, on the paths we roam,
Fortune's soft glow leads us safely home.

Under starlit skies, with courage we cherish,
Crafting our destinies, our fears we will perish.
The glow of fortune, a beacon of light,
Guiding our hearts through the depths of the night.

In the realm of the fables, where magic is spun,
Every shadow and whisper tells how we've begun.
So heed the old tales, for in them we find,
The glow of all fortune, forever entwined.

## Celestial Harvests from the Dragon's Lair

In the depths of the mountain, dragons do sleep,
Guardians of treasures, secrets they keep.
With scales like the stars and breath of pure fire,
Celestial harvests, our hearts they inspire.

Through caverns of wonder, we venture with care,
To dance with the shadows that linger and stare.
In the heart of the lair, where the brave dare to tread,
Whispers of magic surround those who've fled.

The glow of their treasure, a sight to behold,
Glimmers of gemstones, both brilliant and bold.
Each sparkle a promise, a legacy vast,
Harvests of dreams from the dragon's strong grasp.

With courage, we gather the riches of night,
Lighting the way with our hopes burning bright.
Celestial harvests, like dreams from the sky,
Beyond the horizon, where wishes can fly.

So heed the brave tales, let your spirit ignite,
For the dragon's warm glow is a treasure in sight.
Embrace the adventure, let your dreams soar and dare,
To gather the harvests from the dragon's lair.

# Fortunes Woven with Fiery Passion

In the forge of the heart, where desires ignite,
Fortunes are crafted in flames of pure light.
Each ember a wish, each spark a new spark,
Woven with passion, igniting the dark.

From the depths of our souls, the fires will raise,
Forging our futures in bright, hopeful blaze.
With every heartbeat, a rhythm so true,
Fortunes await in the warmth of our view.

In the dance of the fire, we cast out our dreams,
Transforming the shadows with laughter and gleams.
Through trials and triumphs, our passions ignite,
Woven with fortune, we rise to new heights.

Embers of courage scatter through the night,
Guiding us forward, our spirits in flight.
Each thread of our journey, a tapestry bright,
Fiery passions weave fortunes in sight.

So gather your hopes, let your heart take the lead,
For fortunes are woven with love, not with greed.
Embrace every moment, let your spirit prevail,
In the forge of the heart, we'll find our own trail.

# Twisted Golds in Dragon's Embrace

In caverns deep where shadows loom,
The dragon guards its gleaming doom.
Twisted gold with secrets bright,
Spins tales of fire and endless night.

A flicker, a flash, the heart beats fast,
In the echoing dark, the die is cast.
With every word, a bond is made,
In the dance of fate, the debts are paid.

Beneath the wings of ancient lore,
A hidden truth forevermore.
Whispers weave through the smoky air,
Entwining lives in a fateful snare.

Through emerald scales, the light cascades,
Reflecting dreams in shimmering shades.
In this embrace of fire and gold,
Courage blooms and legends unfold.

A treasure sought, yet fraught with dread,
The spirit's call, the heart that bled.
For in the depths where shadows dance,
True courage takes a wondrous chance.

# Harvest of Light in Shadowed Reeds

In twilight's grasp where shadows play,
The reeds whisper secrets of the day.
With every rustle, a tale is spun,
Of dancing hopes beneath the sun.

The river sings with a gentle tune,
Beneath the watch of a silvery moon.
Light filters through in golden strands,
Crafting dreams with delicate hands.

In twilight's glow, the water gleams,
Cradling all our hidden dreams.
Harvest the light, let shadows flee,
Embrace the warmth of what can be.

When echoes linger, time stands still,
The heart knows well its secret thrill.
In every rush, the laughter flows,
In the calm of night, the wild heart grows.

Through the shadowed reeds, adventures rise,
A tapestry woven under open skies.
With each soft whisper, destinies weave,
In the harvest of light, we dare believe.

# Luminous Hopes in the Serpent's Keep

In depths of night where serpent glides,
Hope glimmers bright, though danger hides.
A flickering flame against the chill,
Promises linger, a steadfast will.

Beneath the scales, a heartbeat's song,
Echoes softly where dreams belong.
In shadows cast by glittering eyes,
Lies a world where the brave shall rise.

The darkness whispers of ancient lore,
Paths entwined on forgotten shore.
With every step, a chance to find,
The luminous hopes that fate entwined.

For every curse, a blessing lies,
In this serpent's keep, the spirit flies.
Through winding paths of mystery's art,
A journey leads to the daring heart.

As dawn breaks forth, the shadows fade,
Embracing light, the fears betrayed.
In the serpent's keep, the brave depart,
With luminous hopes, a daring heart.

# Threads of Sunlight in Emerald Fields

Where emerald fields meet azure skies,
Threads of sunlight dance and rise.
Each blade of grass, a story told,
In nature's quilt, stitched with gold.

Breezes carry laughter far and wide,
Through blooming petals, the joy can't hide.
In every hue, the dreams unfold,
Whispers of wishes in colors bold.

The gentle sway in warm embrace,
Encourages hearts to find their place.
With every trot of joyful feet,
In sunlight's grasp, the world feels sweet.

Under the arch of boughs serene,
The magic pulses, alive and keen.
Each day unfolds like a fable spun,
In emerald fields, the adventure's begun.

As stars emerge in twilight's grace,
Threads of sunlight leave their trace.
In dreams woven through the gentle breeze,
Forever cherished, the heart finds ease.

## Bursts of Light in the Dragon's Cradle

In the heart of shadows, where whispers dwell,
Flickers of magic weave spells to tell.
Scaled guardians stir, their eyes aglow,
Guarding the secrets that time won't bestow.

Crimson flames dance in a moonlit night,
Echoes of courage in fierce, brave flight.
Scales shimmer bright under stars' soft gleam,
In the cradle of dragons, we chase a dream.

Ancient runes carved on the stones of fate,
Tell of lost heroes who defied their weight.
In echoes of laughter, we find our way,
Through trials and battles, we dare not sway.

A tapestry woven of starlight and fear,
Each thread holds a promise, a wish, a tear.
As dawn steals the night, the colors ignite,
In the dragon's cradle, we find our light.

## Grains of Luster Amidst the Thorns

In a garden of shadows, where thistles grow,
Bloom fragile petals, in the twilight's glow.
Amongst the sharp whispers, a beauty so rare,
Grains of luster emerge, with stories to share.

Beneath every thorn, a secret is sown,
Echoing tales of the seeds that were thrown.
Golden hues linger on the edges of flight,
Painting the darkness with moments of light.

Sunrise brings whispers of dew-kissed resolve,
As the heart of the garden begins to evolve.
Through trials of nature, the brave shall arise,
Forging a path under vast, open skies.

With laughter like raindrops, the blossoms will sway,
Uniting the sorrows that once led us astray.
In a world full of thorns, may our spirits ignite,
Finding grains of luster, embracing the light.

## Reflective Dews on a Canvas of Dreams

At daybreak, the world sparkles anew,
With reflective dews glistening like dew.
Each drop holds a story, a whisper, a sigh,
Painting the moment as clouds drift by.

A canvas unfolds with colors so bright,
As dreams intertwine, taking glorious flight.
In the heart of the morning, hope starts to bloom,
Chasing away shadows, dispelling the gloom.

The strength of the dreamers weaves through the air,
In a dance of brilliance, free from despair.
Through valleys and mountains, our spirits ascend,
Creating a tapestry that never shall end.

As sunlight cascades on this magical place,
Each creature awakens, filled with such grace.
In the silence of wonder, may our hearts gleam,
Finding reflective dews on the canvas of dreams.

# Hidden Treasures in the Weaver's Keep

In a realm woven tight with stories and threads,
Whispers of magic drift softly like beds.
Hidden treasures lie in the webs spun with care,
Sewn with the love that lingers in air.

Every knot is a memory, a secret to find,
A tapestry woven, so intricately entwined.
The weaver's hands dance, crafting fate's soft embrace,
Bestowing on dreams a most wondrous grace.

With fibers of laughter and echoes of night,
A legacy blossoms, both fragile and bright.
In the heart of this keep, we gather our gold,
Stories of wisdom, forever retold.

As twilight enfolds us, the magic will keep,
Awakening wonders that drift into sleep.
In this sacred space, may our spirits release,
Finding hidden treasures, immersed in peace.

## Golden Seeds Beneath the Scales

In shadows deep where secrets lie,
Golden seeds bask, dreaming high.
Beneath the scales, a story spins,
Of whispered hopes and quiet sins.

They twinkle in the twilight's glow,
Mysteries wrapped in the undertow.
Each chosen spark, a fable's flare,
Cast in the night, breathing air.

With every seed a journey formed,
Through trials faced, the heart transformed.
In endless night where fears take flight,
The golden dreams ignite the night.

So gather round, let tales unfurl,
Of golden seeds that twist and whirl.
In every heart, let courage feed,
Awake the magic, plant the seed.

## Whispered Gold in the Weaving of Tales

In a glen where fairies dance,
Whispered gold ignites a chance.
In every thread, a world is spun,
Stories woven, never done.

With silver moons and starlit beams,
The fabric of our wildest dreams.
Each gentle touch, a tale retold,
Of hearts entwined and destinies bold.

Listen close to the night's embrace,
Where every shadow finds its place.
Each whispered word, a magic spell,
In the weaver's hands, they softly dwell.

So craft your dreams, let courage rise,
Through whispered gold, find new skies.
In every tale, let wonder bloom,
And guide us through the mystic gloom.

## Sunlit Kernels on a Mystic Loom

Underneath the vibrant sun,
Kernels gleam, their journey begun.
On a loom where fate entwines,
Tales of joy and endless signs.

With threads of truth, we stitch our lore,
Every heartbeat, every score.
In sunlit fields, adventures rise,
Carved in whispers of the skies.

From kernel to bloom, the pathway flows,
Each flicker sparks what every heart knows.
A tapestry rich with colors bright,
Guiding dreams through day and night.

So let your spirit soar and gleam,
Beneath the sun, build your dream.
In whispered winds, let stories loom,
A dance of hopes will banish gloom.

## The Glimmering Hearts of Enchanted Threads

In the heart of the ancient glade,
Where enchanted threads begin to fade.
Glimmering hearts, like stars they shine,
Each pulse a note, each beat divine.

With silken whispers, tales ignite,
Chasing shadows, welcoming light.
In every knot, a promise made,
In every fiber, dreams cascaded.

Together we weave through the night,
In the fabric of hope, we find our light.
Glimmering hearts, a bond so pure,
Through tangled paths, our souls endure.

So weave with me in this enchanted space,
Where stories linger, and dreams embrace.
With every thread, let courage rise,
In glimmering hearts, no longing dies.

# Illuminated Beads in the Dancer's Veil

In twilight's hush, the dancers twirl,
With beads aglow, their magic unfurl.
A whisper floats, like dreams on the breeze,
Each movement a story, each turn a tease.

The soft silk shimmers, as shadows blend,
With every step, the night they bend.
Illuminated laughter fills the air,
In a waltz of secrets, beyond compare.

Beneath the stars, they weave their thread,
With colors bright, where none dare tread.
A tapestry woven, of joy and despair,
Each bead a promise, each glance a prayer.

Time lingers here, in a silken embrace,
Where dreams and reality find their place.
With hearts aglow, they dance through the dark,
In the glow of the beads, they leave their mark.

So join the dance, let your spirit flame,
In the glowing night, lose yourself in the game.
For in the veil, the magic resides,
In the illuminated beads, life abides.

## Gold-Laced Secrets of Twilight Tales

In shadows deep, where whispers lie,
The tales of twilight softly sigh.
Gold-laced secrets in the dimmest light,
Ballet of dreams in the velvet night.

Amidst ancient trees, they softly speak,
Of long-lost wishes and futures bleak.
With stories told in hushed refrain,
The echoes linger, like gentle rain.

Through winding paths, the secrets call,
To those who listen, they'll never fall.
Each word a treasure, wrapped in gold,
A tapestry woven from the bold.

The night is alive with the weight of lore,
As stars shimmer bright on the forest floor.
With every heartbeat, the secrets thrive,
In the quiet moments, alight, alive.

So gather 'round, let the stories unfold,
In the dance of twilight, let your heart be bold.
For within the shadows, the gold shall gleam,
In every twilight tale, lies a dream.

# The Fabric of Stars in a Celestial Dance

In a cosmic waltz, the stars align,
Spinning softly, a design divine.
The fabric of night, woven in grace,
A celestial tapestry, time can't erase.

Whispers of stardust drift through the air,
Each twist of fate, a spark of rare.
In the moon's embrace, the universe sighs,
As galaxies swirl, like lullabies.

Light years away, love stories bloom,
In the vast expanse, amidst the gloom.
The dance of the cosmos, a grand parade,
Where memories linger and dreams cascade.

With every heartbeat, the stars ignite,
Drawing shadows from depths into light.
A rhythm eternal, a pulse of the night,
In the fabric of stars, all is right.

So gaze at the heavens, let your heart soar,
In the celestial dance, forevermore.
For every moment holds a spark of chance,
In the fabric of stars, life's eternal dance.

## Glimpses of Gold in the Cunning Shadows

In cunning shadows, gold glimmers bright,
A dance of deception in flickering light.
With secrets concealed in the folds of the night,
Glimpses of treasures out of sight.

The whispers slither through the air,
Like silk in the wind, with impish flair.
Every corner turned, a riddle to seek,
In the heart of the dark, the daring peak.

Gold glints through the veil of obscure,
A beckoning promise, alluring and sure.
With tender steps, the heart starts to race,
In the cunning shadows, find your place.

So tread with caution, yet dare to believe,
In the quest for gold, there's much to achieve.
For in each shadow, the sweet secrets play,
With glimpses of gold leading the way.

As dawn approaches, the shadows will fade,
But the gold will remain, forever arrayed.
In the dance of the night, let hope reside,
In the cunning shadows, dreams shall abide.

### The Spun Silk of Sunlit Harvests

In fields where golden grains do sway,
The whispers of the breeze convey,
Secrets of the sunlit days,
And dreams that dance in nature's play.

Beneath the sky, so vast and blue,
Life weaves a tale, both old and new,
Each harvest speaks of bounteous grace,
A timeless bond in nature's embrace.

The earth a canvas, rich and bright,
Painted with colors, pure delight,
In every seed, a promise sown,
In every heart, a love well-known.

With every dawn, a story grows,
Of laughter found where sunlight flows,
The spun silk threads of day ignite,
A tapestry of pure delight.

As evening falls, the stars arise,
The harvest's glow beneath the skies,
In twilight's hush, the magic swells,
In spun silk dreams, the heart compels.

# Glorifying the Splendor of Sol

Oh, mighty Sol, in radiant flight,
Your golden beams dispel the night,
With every rise, you paint the air,
A canvas bright, beyond compare.

The flowers bloom in your warm embrace,
Life awakens at your gracious pace,
Each dewdrop glistens, thanking you,
For every shade of green and blue.

Your laughter echoes in the breeze,
In whispered tones beneath the trees,
You guide the birds to sing their song,
In perfect harmony, they belong.

Oft have we gathered 'neath your glow,
In fields of joy where wildflowers grow,
With grateful hearts, we lift our voice,
In celebration, we rejoice.

As shadows chase the setting sun,
We thank you for the day now done,
In twilight's arms, we find our rest,
In glorified moments, truly blessed.

# Secrets Buried in Celestial Fabric

In midnight's cloak, the stars conspire,
To weave their tales in waltzing fire,
Each glimmer holds a secret bright,
Within the fabric of the night.

Ancient whispers in the air,
Galaxies dance with elegance rare,
They tell of worlds both near and far,
In dreams adorned with a silver star.

The moon, a keeper of the lore,
Guides lost souls to the distant shore,
Her gentle light a beckoning sign,
To realms where fantasy entwines.

Beneath the heavens, hearts take flight,
Chasing wonders hidden from sight,
With every breath, the cosmos hums,
In spite of silence, magic comes.

Secrets spun in celestial art,
Unraveling slowly, a work of heart,
In the depths of night, we find our peace,
As starlit truths in stillness cease.

## Beneath the Dragon's Glistening Veil

In shadows deep, where legends lie,
Beneath the dragon's watchful eye,
The treasure's guarded, fierce and bold,
In glistening scales of green and gold.

A whisper calls from caverns low,
Where mysteries of ages flow,
With every flicker of candlelight,
The dragons dance, both fierce and bright.

Each tale a tapestry of fire,
Woven with threads of fierce desire,
Of brave adventurers, hearts so true,
Bound by the magic that they pursue.

Through winding paths, the quest unfolds,
With courage forged in ancient holds,
For every shadow hides a chance,
To break the chains, to brave the dance.

As dawn creeps in with softest grace,
The dragon bows, a proud embrace,
In dreams we soar, where wonders dwell,
Forever held beneath the veil.

## Golden Seeds Beneath the Flame

In the twilight's gentle hold,
Golden seeds of dreams unfold.
Whispers dance on warming breeze,
Stories woven among the trees.

Firelight flickers, shadows play,
Magic lingers, night turns day.
With every heartbeat, hopes believe,
In the light, we dare to weave.

Beneath the stars, where wishes gleam,
Hold the light of every dream.
Nurtured by the amber glow,
Futures hidden, yet they grow.

Through the ashes, embers rise,
Sweeping forth a dusky sigh.
Each spark a tale of love and loss,
In every fire, we find the gloss.

For in the heart of flames that burn,
Golden seeds, our fate discern.
In every glow, a journey starts,
Beneath the flame, we guard our hearts.

# A Whisper Among Saffron Threads

In a meadow kissed by sun,
Where saffron threads and shadows run,
A whisper sighs through fields of gold,
Secrets old, yet still untold.

Breezes carry tales of yore,
Softly weaving, evermore.
Petals dance with tender grace,
In their sway, our dreams embrace.

Among the blooms, a promise lies,
Veiled in hues of summer skies.
With every rustle, hearts align,
In whispered truths, our hopes entwine.

Glimmers of fate in verdant thread,
Stories of the lost, the dead.
A tapestry of light and shade,
In nature's hands, our fears are laid.

So let the whispers guide the way,
Through the garden's bright display.
In every sigh, a world anew,
Beneath the threads, take flight and flew.

# Secrets of the Sunlit Grove

In the grove where daylight beams,
Life awakens, dances, dreams.
Whispers linger on the air,
Secrets wrapped in silence fair.

Leaves of emerald sway above,
Guarding stories, tales of love.
Sunlight dapples, shadows weave,
In this haven, hearts believe.

Ancient trees in wisdom stand,
Roots entwined in timeless land.
Each rustling leaf a gentle sigh,
Carried forth on breezes high.

Among the branches, hopes take flight,
In every glimmer, magic's light.
Where dreams unfurl, and spirits mend,
In sunlit paths, we find our friend.

With every secret the grove imparts,
We become the sum of parts.
Nature whispers, and we know,
In the sunlit grove, our lives will grow.

# Jewel Tones in the Looming Shadows

In shadows deep, where whispers dwell,
Jewel tones cast a vibrant spell.
Emerald greens and sapphire blues,
Weaving paths where dreams infuse.

Each hue a story, rich and rare,
Echoes linger in the air.
In twilight's dance, a soft embrace,
The looming shadows find their place.

Glimmers flash in dusk's cascade,
Secrets shimmer, never fade.
Through the dark, a radiance glows,
In every heart, a tale bestows.

With every breath, the colors sway,
Painting night, enchanting day.
In this realm of light and shade,
A tapestry of dreams is laid.

So linger here, where magic thrives,
In jewel tones, where spirit strives.
Beneath the shadows, whispers beam,
In every color, find your dream.

# Echoes of the Gilded Realm

In shadows cast by golden beams,
A whisper floats through ancient dreams.
The walls remember tales of yore,
Where hearts once danced on emerald floor.

Amidst the echoes, secrets sigh,
Beneath the watchful, starry sky.
Old spirits waltz with gentle grace,
In every corner, time's embrace.

The gilded realm, a fleeting glance,
With magic woven in each chance.
Hold tight the moments pure and bright,
As day retreats, surrender night.

The air is thick with silent prayers,
Voices linger, light as airs.
With every breath, the past ignites,
In twilight's glow, the heart delights.

Through gilded halls, the shadows roam,
In their embrace, we find our home.
A tapestry of laughter and tears,
Echoes of joy throughout the years.

# Where Light Kisses the Tapestry

Where light weaves through the velvet night,
In colors bold, in soft delight.
Threads of magic, bright and pure,
A tapestry, forever sure.

In every corner, stories glow,
As starlight whispers tales below.
The fabric hums with dreams and wishes,
Where hope resides and joy replenishes.

The dance of shadows, swift and true,
Draws patterns bold in sapphire hue.
Within each weave, a heartbeat sings,
Of timeless loves and wondrous things.

Oh, to embrace the woven grace,
Where light and shadow meet in space.
A sanctuary for the heart,
An artful world, a sacred part.

As dawn approaches, colors fade,
Yet in our hearts, the dreams are laid.
For in the night, our spirits play,
Where light kisses the tapestry sway.

## The Bursting Essence of Dawn


Awakening the world with light,
The bursting essence, pure and bright.
With every ray, the shadows flee,
A symphony of hope, wild and free.

Golden fingers touch the dew,
Painting skies in shades anew.
Each moment tugs at slumber's heart,
Inviting life to take its part.

As blossoms stretch in gentle grace,
The morning sings, a warm embrace.
The world exults in splendor's show,
As day breaks forth, a vibrant glow.

The air is laced with fragrant cheer,
A tender promise, drawing near.
With every heartbeat, time unlocks,
In dawn's embrace, the world unblocks.

So let us dance beneath the sun,
Embracing all that's yet to come.
For in this burst of golden dawn,
Our dreams take flight, forever drawn.

# Fruits of the Fiery Aether

In realms where flame and spirit dance,
The fruits of aether spark romance.
With every ember, stories blend,
A vivid tale that knows no end.

The sky ablaze with colors rare,
A canvas painted with heart and care.
Each flicker holds a secret's light,
In passionate whispers of the night.

Through swirling mist and jeweled air,
The fiery essence lingers there.
With every breath, the magic swells,
In tales of love, the heart compels.

To taste the sweetness, take a chance,
Let passion lead the timeless dance.
For in this realm, the wild meets wise,
Where fiery dreams ignite the skies.

So pluck the fruits, let spirit soar,
Embrace the aether forevermore.
In this bright world, our souls will sing,
The fruits of fire, a wondrous thing.

## The Radiance Tucked in Every Fold

In whispers soft, the secrets hide,
Beneath the layers, dreams abide.
Each crease a story, gently spun,
Unraveling light, where shadows run.

With every touch, a spark ignites,
In twilight's grasp, the heart excites.
The fabric glows with hopes untold,
A tapestry of warmth and bold.

Fate stitched within the seams so fine,
A woven path, a secret line.
In every fold, the magic swirls,
A dance of colors, life unfurls.

Look closely, see the mysteries blend,
In endless layers, dreams extend.
The fabric speaks of worlds unseen,
A radiant quilt of all that's been.

So hold it close, let shadows fade,
Embrace the light, the hope displayed.
For in each fold, a wonder lies,
The radiance that never dies.

# Cunning Threads of Gold in Gossamer Winds

In golden threads, the truth does weave,
A tapestry of what we believe.
Each gust of wind, a tale to tell,
Of whispered vows, in silence dwell.

Cunning stitches in twilight's glow,
A flicker of fate in every flow.
Gossamer dreams in the evening breeze,
Entwine with the stars, a cosmic tease.

Through branches high, the secrets drift,
Carried away like a precious gift.
Every shimmer, a soft embrace,
Threads of gold in a tangled chase.

As night descends, the magic sings,
With every sigh, the starlight clings.
In hushed tones, the stories unfold,
In gossamer winds, the threads turn bold.

So let them guide you, through shadowed glades,
With cunning paths, the heart invades.
For in the night, each thread takes flight,
Woven with dreams that feel so right.

## Celestial Gleam on the Edge of Night

When twilight falls, the stars appear,
A celestial dance, so bright and clear.
Each spark a promise, a wish on high,
Glimmers of hope as the day says goodbye.

On the edge of night, where shadows slide,
The moon whispers softly, secrets abide.
A gleam of silver, a guiding light,
Painting the world in ethereal sight.

Amongst the silence, the dreams take shape,
In the velvet dark, the heart escapes.
Celestial echoes fill the air,
Inviting the lost, beckoning care.

With every twinkle, the night reveals,
A tapestry of what the heart feels.
In the hush of dusk, the magic flows,
Each celestial gleam, a love that grows.

So look to the stars when shadows fall,
In their radiant glow, you'll hear the call.
For on the edge of night's soft sigh,
Lies the promise of dreams that'll never die.

# Secrets of Gold in the Serpent's Grove

In the serpent's grove, where shadows linger,
Golden secrets pulse, a charmed finger.
Beneath the branches, whispers play,
In the rustling leaves, the night holds sway.

Curved paths weave through a world unknown,
Where every heartbeat feels like home.
The air shimmers with tales untold,
In the serpent's embrace, treasure unfolds.

Glimmers of gold in the forest deep,
Guarding the dreams that memories keep.
Each rustle speaks of ancient grace,
In every shadow, a warm embrace.

In twilight's sigh, the secrets bloom,
Revealing the magic in every room.
The serpent winds through realms of time,
In golden echoes, a whispered rhyme.

So step with care in the grove tonight,
For in its heart, you'll find the light.
Secrets of gold waiting to be found,
In the magic of the serpent's sound.

# The Gilded Nest of Forgotten Echoes

In the heart of shadows deep,
Whispers of the past will creep,
Nestled where the lost dreams lay,
Gilded tales of yesterday.

Amongst the leaves a secret hides,
A place where time and truth abides,
Echoes call from ages worn,
A memory of worlds reborn.

Forgotten paths come into view,
In twilight's charm, the old feels new,
With every step on ancient stone,
The gilded nest feels like home.

Winds of fate swiftly will weave,
Stories only souls believe,
In the quiet, magic stirs,
Where each echo softly purrs.

Embrace the light, let shadows die,
Gilded hopes in the evening sky,
Within this nest, the heart will rest,
In forgotten tunes, we are blessed.

# Ethereal Currents in a World of Threads

Woven dreams in twilight's grace,
Threads of magic, time and space,
Ethereal currents, soft and bright,
Guide the hearts through endless night.

In every strand, a secret flows,
Stories told where the river goes,
Tangled whispers call us near,
To worlds where hope and love adhere.

With gentle hands, we spin the tale,
Through lands of light, we will not fail,
Each thread a wish, a spark, a fire,
Ethereal currents lift us higher.

In the loom of fate, we find our way,
A tapestry that none can fray,
In each knot, a dream we thread,
Through the world's embrace, we're led.

So dance along the woven line,
In this journey, hearts entwine,
For in the world of threads so rare,
Ethereal echoes fill the air.

## Radiant Journeys through Golden Waters

Upon the lake where sunlight gleams,
Golden waters cradle dreams,
A radiant path unfolds ahead,
With whispers soft, the journey's led.

Through ripples bright, the visions flow,
Casting light on stories slow,
Each wave a promise, gently sways,
In the heart of nature's praise.

Sail upon hope's brilliant tide,
With courage as your faithful guide,
Journey forth where warmth ignites,
Through golden waters, day and night.

Every splash a laughter's song,
In joyful streams, we all belong,
Radiant echoes, as they soar,
Carry us to distant shore.

Let all your worries drift away,
In golden hues, we'll find our way,
For every journey has its start,
With radiant love, we'll chart the heart.

# The Dance of Gold in Celestial Realms

In twilight's breath, the stars align,
A golden dance of fate divine,
Celestial realms where dreams take flight,
Illuminate the velvet night.

With every twirl, the cosmos hums,
A symphony where starlight drums,
The whispers of the universe,
In sparkling notes, the heavens burst.

To revel in this astral waltz,
Where even silence holds no faults,
In golden threads of time and space,
We dance with joy, we find our place.

Each galaxy a shimmering guide,
Through the darkness, we will glide,
In celestial realms, the magic sways,
A dance of gold in endless praise.

So join the leap, embrace the glow,
In the dance of gold, together flow,
Through night and dawn, we shall perform,
In celestial realms, love keeps us warm.

# Enchanted Weave Beneath the Winged Sun

In a glade where shadows play,
Whispers weave the light of day.
Threads of magic, soft and bright,
Dance like fireflies in the night.

Breezes hum a cheerful tune,
Echoed by the rising moon.
Nature's secrets softly gleam,
Woven tightly like a dream.

Petals blush with morning grace,
While the sunbeams kiss their face.
Here in this enchanted glen,
Time stands still, and hearts begin.

Murmurs of the ancient trees,
Carried on the gentle breeze.
In their halls, the stories call,
Beneath the sun, a magic thrall.

So let your spirit wander free,
Where the heart knows harmony.
In this place, forever stay,
Among the light, the magic play.

# Tales Unfurled with Sparks of Light

In twilight's glow, the stories rise,
Beneath the canvas of the skies.
With every spark, a tale takes flight,
Unraveling dreams with pure delight.

The phoenix sings, its voice so clear,
In whispered tones, we hold it dear.
Each line a dance, a flicker bright,
Igniting souls with pure insight.

Through valleys deep and mountains high,
Adventures sprout, unfold, and sigh.
With every heartbeat, tales are spun,
As mysteries twine, we come undone.

Creatures dance in shadow's grace,
The stars illuminate their place.
In every corner, treasure found,
In whispers soft, their voices sound.

So gather 'round and share the night,
With stories woven, hearts alight.
For every truth, a spark shall glow,
As tales unfurl in evening's flow.

# The Dragon's Heartbeats Beneath the Vine

Underneath the tangled vine,
Dragon spirits softly shine.
With every thrum, the earth does quake,
In their heartbeat, wonders wake.

Glimmers flash in emerald hue,
Wings unfold, a sight so new.
Guardians of the forest deep,
They safeguard secrets, never sleep.

With fiery breath and gentle grace,
They dance through time, they weave through space.
In the shadows, whispers call,
Echoing through the great hall.

Beneath the stars, their tales are spun,
In the twilight, battles won.
From ancient dreams, they rise anew,
In every heart, their spirit grew.

So when you hear a distant roar,
Feel the magic at your door.
For in each roar, a heartbeat beats,
A dragon's love forever greets.

# Shimmering Harvest Binding Souls Together

In fields of gold where dreams take flight,
Harvest whispers in the night.
Glistening grains, like stars that gleam,
Binding souls in a timeless dream.

With every hand that gathers grain,
The laughter mingles with the pain.
Echoes of both joy and sorrow,
Crafting hope for a new tomorrow.

Ripened fruit beneath the sun,
Echoes of the work once done.
Each grain a story, each seed a prayer,
Nurtured with love, beyond compare.

As twilight falls, the hearth ignites,
Embers dance with friendly lights.
Families gather, hearts entwined,
In every harvest, love we find.

The shimmer speaks of bonds so strong,
Where every soul can feel they belong.
In this bounty, let us see,
The strength in unity, wild and free.

## The Enchanted Harvest's Embrace

In fields of gold where shadows play,
The harvest sings in hues of gray.
A gentle breeze, a whispered call,
Beneath the boughs, we gather all.

The pumpkins glow like lanterns bright,
As twilight dances on the night.
With hands entwined, we lift our gaze,
To claim the blessings of our days.

The moon beholds our joyful song,
In unity, we all belong.
Amongst the corn, our laughter soars,
In this embrace, forevermore.

With every step, the earth, it sighs,
A realm enchanted, 'neath the skies.
Each whispered promise, soft and sweet,
Guides weary souls to rest their feet.

The harvest moon, a watchful eye,
As dancing shadows pass us by.
In whispered winds, our stories share,
In love and light, beyond compare.

# Echoes of Gilded Whispers

In the silence of the golden morn,
Echoes whisper tales reborn.
From ancient trees, their secrets spill,
Softly humming, time stands still.

A world adorned in autumn's fire,
Where dreams converge, and hearts conspire.
Through rustling leaves, a voice so sweet,
We join the whispers, pulse and beat.

Beneath the sun's embrace, we tread,
With fleeting hopes, our spirits fed.
In shimmering light, we find our way,
As gilded dreams refuse to fray.

In twilight's glow, the shadows weave,
A tapestry of hearts that believe.
With every sigh, the night awakes,
And through the dark, a new dawn breaks.

So linger here in fleeting grace,
With every heartbeat, time's embrace.
In echoes soft, our stories blend,
A gilded journey, without end.

# Beneath the Dragon's Gaze

Upon the peaks where eagles soar,
A dragon watches, wise and sure.
With emerald eyes, it guards the skies,
Revealing truth in ancient sighs.

In caverns deep, where shadows play,
The whispers of the fierce display.
Of battles fought and legends made,
In fiery breath, our fears allayed.

Through clouds of mist, a tale unfolds,
Of dreams untold and hearts of gold.
Beneath its gaze, we learn to fly,
Embracing wonders, reaching high.

The night ignites with gleams of fire,
With every roar, our souls aspire.
In scales of dusk, the stars align,
And forge a path where fate entwines.

So heed the dragon's watchful eye,
For through its strength, we'll learn to try.
In daring hearts and valiant themes,
We chase the light, we chase our dreams.

# Threads of Radiant Essence

In tapestry of night, we thread,
The colors of our dreams, unsaid.
With every stitch, a story spun,
A world awakened, one by one.

The silken strands of hope we weave,
In patterns bold, we dare believe.
With gentle hands, the essence glows,
In every heart, a garden grows.

The dawn arrives, in shimmers bright,
Awakening the magic light.
Each whisper shared, a fragrant bloom,
In vibrant hues that chase all gloom.

With sunlit threads, we bravely start,
The journey beckons, calls each heart.
In woven dreams, our spirits dance,
Embracing fate, we seize the chance.

So gather close, in radiant threads,
With every turn, our spirit spreads.
In unity, we shape the night,
Together crafting pure delight.

# The Golden Veins of Twilight

Whispers of dusk weave through the air,
Golden seams in the sky so rare.
A shimmer of dreams on the wind's frail sigh,
As stars ignite in the gathering high.

Soft shadows dance on the breath of the night,
Where magic stirs in the fading light.
Secrets curl like leaves on the ground,
In this twilight realm, true wonders abound.

Crimson and amber weave tales of old,
Of heroes and spirits, both brave and bold.
Each shimmering moment, a fleeting embrace,
The beauty of time cannot be replaced.

Glimmers of hope in the twilight glow,
Illuminate paths where the dreamers go.
With each heartbeat, the world starts to sing,
A symphony born on the footsteps of spring.

So linger awhile in the sweet dusky charm,
Let go of your worries, let love be your balm.
For in the soft dusk where the magic is spun,
The golden veins of twilight have just begun.

## Lush Gifts from Shadowed Fields

In the stillness where whispers reside,
A bounty of secrets the shadows confide.
Fields woven green by the hands of the earth,
Each blade and each bloom sing of their worth.

With dew-kissed petals, the morning unfolds,
Stories of ancient enchantment retold.
Each gust of the breeze carries laughter and cheer,
From the heart of the shadows, sweet gifts appear.

Soft silences cradle the shimmering night,
Where creatures of wonder take graceful flight.
The rustle of leaves tells of dreams that await,
In the lush, hidden realms where the passions create.

Moonlight cascades over fields bathed in gloom,
Painting the dark with a hint of perfume.
Each echo of nature sings deep in the soul,
Bringing together what once felt too whole.

So wander this magic, embrace the unknown,
For the lush gifts of shadow are truly your own.
In every soft sigh, in each playful yield,
Life's sweetest treasures lie in these fields.

## A Dance with Celestial Spoils

Under a canvas of twilight's embrace,
The cosmos twirls in a fateful dance space.
Stars tiptoe softly, a celestial ball,
Each glimmer a wish, a beckon, a call.

With constellations stitching tales in the night,
Their stories immortalized with pure light.
Planets cartwheel through the velvet expanse,
Inviting the dreamers to join in their dance.

Amongst the soft clouds, the moon winks in glee,
With shadows of dreams cradling you and me.
Galaxies spin with a whisper of grace,
Drawing our hearts to their magical place.

In this sacred moment, as time softly sways,
We twirl with the stardust, lost in the blaze.
With every heartbeat, the universe glows,
A dance with celestial spoils, one forever knows.

So reach for the heavens, let the night fill your heart,
For in this cosmic rhythm, we each play a part.
In the dance of existence, where spirits take flight,
The universe calls us to wander its night.

# Radiance in the Clutches of Myth

Amidst the enigma where legends are born,
Radiance flickers, yet never is worn.
Myths wrapped in shadows, with glimmers of gold,
Tell stories of bravery, both tender and bold.

From the depths of the sea to the heights of the sky,
Creatures of wonder, on whispers, they fly.
Each tale a brushstroke on time's endless scroll,
In the clutches of myth, we uncover our soul.

A phoenix rises from ashes of grief,
Illuminating darkness, a promise of belief.
Elves dance in moonlight, their laughter, a song,
Inviting the weary to join them along.

With each passing moment, new stories unfold,
Of courage, of love, and of destinies bold.
In the tapestry woven with threads of delight,
Radiance glimmers, enchanting the night.

So treasure these myths, let their magic ignite,
The courage within you to rise and take flight.
For in the embrace of the stories we share,
Radiance blooms and fills the air.

### Radiant Orbs within the Fiery Tapestry

In twilight's grasp, the orbs ignite,
They dance like stars in velvet night.
A tapestry of hues so bold,
With secrets whispered, dreams unfold.

Beneath their glow, the shadows play,
A fleeting waltz, then drift away.
With every flicker, hope ascends,
As night bestows its calming bends.

Each orb a wish, a heart's desire,
A spark that sets the soul on fire.
They twine in flames of whispered lore,
In radiant light, forevermore.

The world transforms, a painted scheme,
As weaves of magic fill the dream.
The fiery tapestry entwined,
In every heart, its gift designed.

So gaze upon the orbs tonight,
Let them inspire your inner light.
With every glance, a tale you'll find,
In radiant orbs, our fates aligned.

# Glinting Harvests Beneath the Azure Wings

Under the arch of azure skies,
The glinting harvests swiftly rise.
Like golden gems in fields of green,
They shimmer bright, a vibrant scene.

With whispers soft as morning breezes,
The earth awakens, and joy increases.
Each fruit of labor, ripe and true,
A bounty shared by me and you.

Beneath the wings of azure flight,
Life dances in the warm sunlight.
The laughter of the children rings,
In celebration of these things.

A moment grasped, a fleeting smile,
We gather round and stay awhile.
The harvest glimmers, setting free,
Our dreams, like birds, in wild jubilee.

So cherish all the gifts we reap,
In every heart, a story deep.
With glinting harvests, love will sing,
Beneath the vast and azure wing.

## Merging Gleams in a Weaver's Reverie

In twilight's touch, where shadows blend,
A weaver crafts with dreams to send.
Merging gleams of light and dark,
Within her world, she leaves her mark.

Each thread a tale, a winding quest,
The fabric soft, a cozy nest.
With every stitch, a memory sewn,
In whispers soft, her heart is known.

A dance of colors, bold yet shy,
A tapestry that lifts the eye.
Through weft and warp, her visions soar,
In every fiber, legends roar.

As twilight fades, the magic swells,
Her hands weave stories time retells.
Merging gleams with patient grace,
In the weaver's dream, we find our place.

So let us flow through dreams tonight,
Embrace the colors, bask in light.
For in her reverie, we unite,
In merging gleams that shine so bright.

## Dappled Golds in the Enchanted Glen

In the enchanted glen, a dance unfolds,
Dappled golds, a beauty bold.
Where sunlight weaves through ancient trees,
And laughter mingles with the breeze.

Each moment sparkles, bright and clear,
A symphony of joy draws near.
The flowers bloom in golden grace,
A treasure found in this embrace.

With every step, the whispers hum,
As nature calls, it's time to come.
To bask beneath the dappled shade,
Where dreams are spun and memories laid.

In twilight's glow, the magic sings,
The gentle rustle of fairy wings.
In dappled light, our spirits soar,
In the enchanted glen, forevermore.

So let your heart be free and roam,
In nature's arms, we find our home.
With dappled golds and wonders grand,
Embrace the magic of this land.

# The Elysian Threads of Myth and Gold

In the loom of dreams, the threads entwine,
Golden whispers dance, in shadows they shine.
Legends stitched with a silken grace,
Elysian tales in this timeless space.

Voices echo through the ancient trees,
Casting spells with the softest breeze.
Each story woven in twilight's glow,
Myth and gold in a radiant flow.

Guided by starlight, the fables ignite,
Glimmers of hope in the velvety night.
Threads of the past, where ages converge,
In this tapestry, dreams gently surge.

A tapestry rich, with secrets untold,
In every stitch, a magic to hold.
Beneath the sky, under moon's gentle care,
Elysian threads shimmer, forever rare.

Through time and space, the stories we weave,
In golden realms, where spirits believe.
The heart of the myth, the pulse of the old,
In this woven dream, our lives unfold.

## The Shining Veil of Olden Stories

Beneath a veil spun from starlit yore,
Whispers of ancients resound evermore.
Echoing laughter in the twilight's embrace,
Olden stories dance with a timeless grace.

A lantern of memories, flickering bright,
Guiding lost souls through the velvet night.
Each tale a treasure, a radiant spark,
Illuminated softly, breaking the dark.

In shadows they linger, the ghosts of the past,
Woven in laughter, in sorrows amassed.
With each whispered legend, the fabric we mend,
In the shining veil, the horizons extend.

Through valleys of silence, their echoes resound,
In the heart of the forest, the stories are found.
A symphony sung by the voices of time,
In the shining veil, every note is a rhyme.

So gather your courage, let tales be your guide,
Through the shimmering veil where shadows reside.
For in olden stories, the magic remains,
A tapestry woven with joy and with pains.

# Flickering Jewels in the Skies of Fate

Upon the canvas of a velvet sky,
Flickering jewels, the dreams that fly.
Each star a promise, a wish yet to bloom,
In the cosmic dance, dispelling the gloom.

Threads of the universe, tangled and bright,
Twinkling with secrets, bathed in soft light.
Navigating pathways where shadows play,
In the skies of fate, the night sings its sway.

Captured in moments, the light starts to weave,
A tapestry glowing in stories conceived.
Mosaic of hopes, where futures align,
Flickering jewels, a celestial sign.

From the depths of silence, the echoes arise,
A chorus of wonders, enchanting the skies.
With each fleeting glimpse, our spirits take flight,
Chasing the flickers, igniting the night.

So lift up your gaze and embrace the unknown,
For within every star, a magic is sown.
In the boundless expanse, where dreams truly rate,
Lie flickering jewels in the skies of fate.

# Ethereal Sun in the Keeper's Hand

In the cavern of wonders, a keeper stands,
Holding an ethereal sun in their hands.
Golden radiance spills like sweet honey,
Threads of warmth twine, glowing like money.

With each gentle pulse, the shadows retreat,
Where light meets the dark, their dance is complete.
The keeper whispers to the day and the night,
Guiding lost dreams back to glittering light.

In the heart of the dawn, where magic begins,
Eternal horizons beckon like winds.
Each beam a promise, each shimmer a chance,
In the keeper's hand, the cosmos will dance.

As twilight descends, when the stars softly rise,
The sun becomes stories that fill up the skies.
In the dance of transition, the essence expands,
With the ethereal sun in the keeper's hands.

So walk with your head held high to the glow,
Embrace all the wonders that life tries to show.
In the keeper's embrace, find courage to stand,
For each heart holds a sun in its gentle hand.

# The Woven Wind Whispering of Glory

In the dance of the leaves, soft whispers play,
Mountains stretch high, where shadows softly sway.
Glory unfolds in the morning's embrace,
As fields blush golden, each flower finds grace.

Breezes carry tales through the age-old trees,
Songs of the ancients, a tapestry of ease.
Stars twinkle gently in the velvet night,
Guiding lost wanderers with shimmering light.

Echoes of laughter on pathways untold,
Where dreams become stories, and hope turns to gold.
The woven winds shift, crafting tales anew,
For those who dare listen, the secrets ensue.

With each rustling sigh, a new tale is spun,
In the heart of the woods, our journeys begun.
Glory is not just in triumphs we find,
But in moments of magic that linger behind.

So let the wind guide you, where wonders abound,
In the silence of night, where new dreams are found.
For every soft whisper is a promise, a plea,
In the woven wind's heart, it's all waiting for thee.

# Dreams Untamed in a Dragon's Heart

In the shadows of night, fierce dreams take their flight,
A dragon awakens, igniting the night.
With scales like the stars, and a fire so bright,
He guards all the dreams that take shape in his sight.

Untamed and unyielding, he roams through the skies,
Chasing the secrets the daylight denies.
His roar shakes the mountains, a symphony grand,
As echoes of power sweep across the land.

Each dream is a treasure, each wish a rare gem,
Crafted in starlight, they belong to him.
With wings like the tempest, he dances on air,
Breathing life into visions, a magical flair.

In the heart of the night, where the wild spirits play,
A dragon guards dreams that sparkle and sway.
For dreams untamed are the legends of old,
Whispered through ages, each story retold.

So ride on the winds of your wildest desire,
Let dreams be the canvas, let passion inspire.
For the heart of a dragon holds power unseen,
In the dance of the cosmos, let your spirit glean.

## The Glistening Threads of Time's Embrace

In a loom of the cosmos, the threads intertwine,
Weaving stories of glory in patterns divine.
Moments like diamonds, they sparkle and gleam,
Caught in the fabric of life's endless dream.

Time whispers softly with glances of fate,
Every heartbeat rises, never too late.
The tapestry shimmers, a dance of delight,
Guided by starlight that pierces the night.

With colors of sunsets and shadows of dawn,
Each thread tells a story, as new days are born.
The whispers of ages echo through space,
Binding our souls in the warmest embrace.

So gather your memories like treasures unfurled,
Each moment a stitch in this wondrous world.
For time, like a river, flows ceaseless and free,
And the glistening threads weave eternity.

In laughter and silence, in joy's gentle balm,
Time wraps its arms 'round you, tender and calm.
Each heartbeat, each sigh, in this grand tapestry,
Crafts the essence of who we're meant to be.

# A Tapestry of Radiance in Dusk

As twilight descends with a whispering sigh,
The world dons its mantle, the stars filling the sky.
A tapestry woven with colors so bold,
In the hush of the evening, every heart it holds.

Shadows stretch long as the sun takes its rest,
Embracing the night in a silken caress.
The moonlight like silver, a soft, gentle beam,
Weaving dreams in the stillness, a magical theme.

In gardens aglow with the fireflies' dance,
Hope shimmers softly, all hearts have a chance.
For dusk is a painter with an artist's delight,
Creating a canvas where dreams take their flight.

With each passing moment, the colors unite,
Crafting serenity, a beautifully bright.
So gather your hopes in the glow of this hour,
As night wraps its cloak around each blooming flower.

Embrace the radiance, let your spirit soar,
For within the tapestry, there's always more.
In the dance of the dusk, where the day meets the night,
Magic awakens, and dreams take to flight.

www.ingramcontent.com/pod-product-compliance
Ingram Content Group UK Ltd.
Pitfield, Milton Keynes, MK11 3LW, UK
UKHW021438220125
4239UKWH00039B/723

9 781805 649694